ISBN: 978-0-9997527-2-2

This book is dedicated to Frank Murphy, David Bowie, Lil Peep, Belle, and all of the vine creators for their wonderful content.

milk and vine II
by adam gasiewski and emily beck

Foreword

In 2011, I reluctantly created a Twitter account. A good friend relentlessly persuaded me to try it. She told me it would be like my public diary, where I could say whatever came to my mind and be as personal as I wanted. Within days, I was sending tweets like "Beat my ass with another Ass." I was having fun online.

In 2013 Vine was open to the public and I wanted absolutely nothing to do with it. People kept saying vine was revolutionary but it just seemed like Twitter but with video time limits. Most of the things I saw there made me cringe. I saw hundreds of uncultured and talentless swine blowing up off of misogynistic, lazy, cheap comedy. Frankly, it was just off-putting. My loyal six fans told me to try it, and after a year of pestering I again downloaded an application I didn't want to.

The whole first year or so of using Vine I refused to show my face, worrying about future employees discovering my online identity. Not to mention I'm an acne covered scum-sucking creature, I didn't go to college, I worked several jobs, and lived on my own in a trash palace. I didn't want to scare away all the hot vine babes.

I eventually opened up online and showed my face, my life, and more of my personal sense of humor. At this time I had a couple thousand followers on Twitter and about 100 on Vine. None of this mattered to me. I had my friends who I made on Twitter and I had friends from school, and all those other talented and wholesome humans who followed me I just didn't give a shit about them. I didn't know these people, I still don't, but if they want to read my tweets or watch my vines that's cool with me.

I woke up one morning, after a long 3 days asleep and sick with the stomach flu, with over 300 notifications from Vine. Thousands of people following me & commenting on my Vines out of completely nowhere. I discovered a small, ever growing community of people making truly hilarious Videos. I loved these people and I found every day I followed more and more talented individuals. Before this I never watched vines because all I was seeing before were things along the lines of "slappin ur girls Ass" directed by fully grown up trust fund babies with the mind still like a teenage boy.

Less than a year later I had made so many friends because of Vine. I visited people I have never met before, and brought these same people into my own home. These were people just like me with regular lives making bullshit 6 second videos for fun. I had hundreds of thousands of followers on Vine and I appreciate all of them supporting me. I always thought it was kind of funny that there were this many people who wanted to look through my public diary and read the thoughts I jotted down. It is also very flattering that they were fine with seeing my small, but plump, bare Ass all the time.

Although I didn't want to join vine, I eventually fell in love with it, and the rest of the people around the world creating content. Vine was a place where I could make 20 vines on my way home from a overnight shift, walking in alleys and vomiting out whatever nonsense came to my brain.

Vine taught me that every single person can capture something beautiful with their camera as long as they're engaged in an easily digestible platform. Everyone can make art, whether it be filming somebody drop their croissant, someone viewing a sunset, or someone slapping cheese singlets on their bare ass. Vine was chill as hell, and without it I'd never have been able to have sex.

– Karl from Online
@HammerFist3

they ask you
how you are
and you just have to say
that you're fine
when
you're not really fine
but you just can't get into it
because they would never

understand.

okay class
let's take roll

um

shithead

it's *shit__head__*

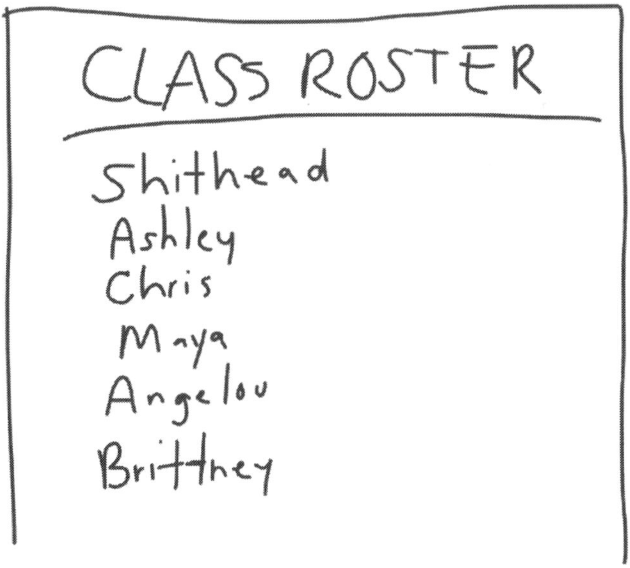

CLASS ROSTER

Shithead
Ashley
Chris
Maya
Angelou
Brittney

i saw you hanging out with
caitlyn
yesterday

re-rebecca
it's not what you think–

i won't hesitate bitch

hey darren

sup bitch

ahha stop

bitch heh

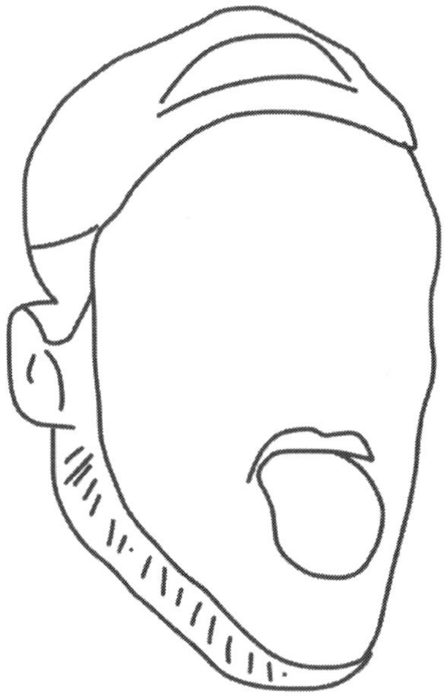

<u>*ahhh*</u>

and they were
<u>roommates</u>

oh my god
they were
<u>roommates</u>

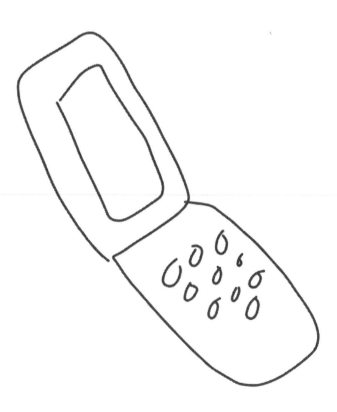

happy birthday raven

i can't swim

hauh, you can't sit with us

actually
megan
i can't sit anywhere
i have

hemorrhoids

fuck
your
chicken strips

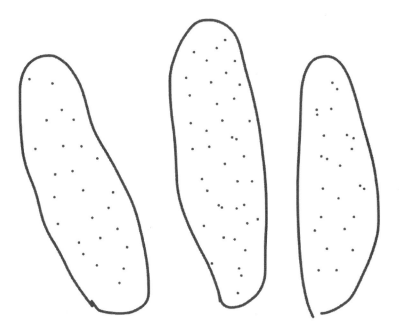

there's only one thing
worse than
a rapist

a child

no

zach
stop
zach stop
you're gonna get in trouble
zach

what the fuck
is this allowed
what the fuck
is that allowed

no not a dresser
yes a dresser
yes
yes
yes
trashcan yes
oh my god

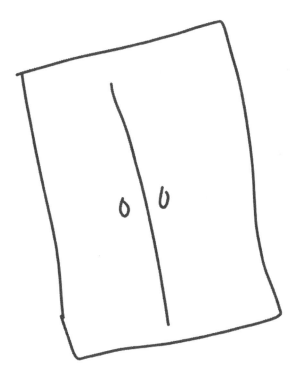

i thought you loved me
you was my baby
my fuckin cinnamon apple

cam and colin
run in here
and come get y'all juice

shit

oh my god
oh my god
he on x games mode

on all levels
except physical
i am a wolf

arf

wow

give me your

fuckin

money

road work ahead
uh
yeah
i sure hope it does

hey everybody
today my brother pushed me
so i'm starting a kickstarter
to put him down
benefits of killing him would be
i would get pushed way less

if your name is junior
and you're really handsome
come on raise your hand

when i leave
you wanna keep
doing this
but then when i come around
you don't wanna
post up

i want a church girl
that go to church
and read her bible

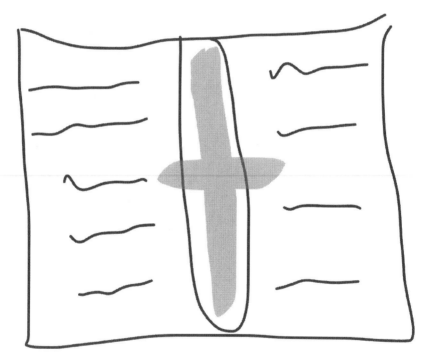

i smell like beef
i smell like beef
i smell like beef

go ahead and introduce yourself

my name is michael
with a b
and i've been afraid of
insects my entire–

stop stop
stop
where
mm
where's the b

there's a bee

you're disrespecting
you're dis
respecting a future
u.s. army soldier

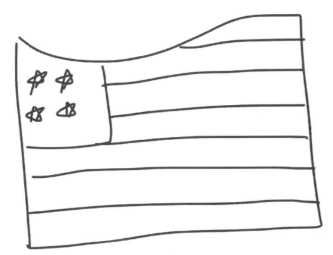

listen to this
one part of this song
wait wait
wait
ready

are you fucking kidding me

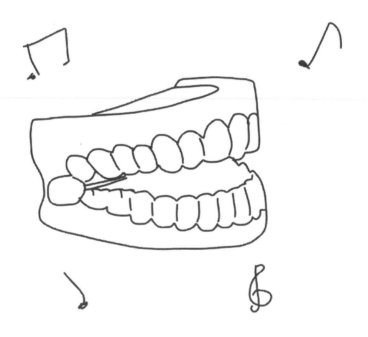

i think i
i think i know more about
american girl dolls
than you do
genius

so i'm sitting there
barbeque sauce
on my titties

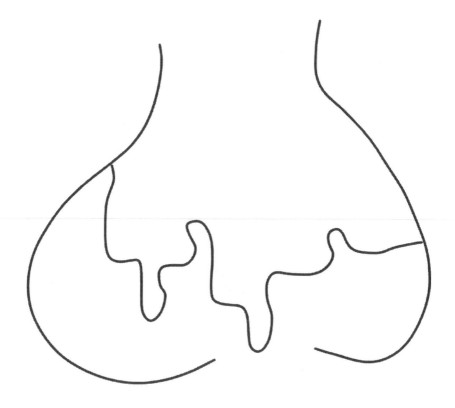

honestly
i don't remember
i was prolly fucked up
yeah
i was crazy back then
heuaheuhah

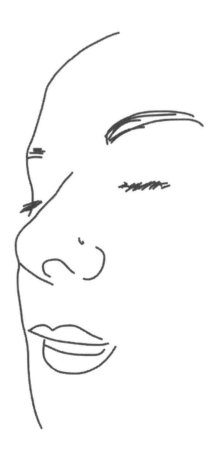

duude
what the fawk
this is your space
this is your areah
she can't do that to
you

omg
i love chipotle
chipotle is my life

bro
can i get a sip of that water

it's not water

vodka
i like your style

it's vinegar

what

it's vinegar
pussy

don't even say nothin to me
boy you look like
a motha fuckin
uhhhhhh

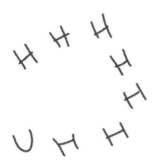

how do you know
if you're gay

why does my penis
grow in the morning

why don't i have a penis

we all die
you either kill yourself
or get killed

whatchu gon do
whatchu gon do

chris
is that a
weed

no
this is a crayon

i'm calling the police

two shots
of
vodka

yes
she is a bitch

b
i
c
t
h

issa fourth of july
i'm ready to
pop these firecrackers
don pop em on me
where da police at

how do you know
what's good for me

*that's my **opinion***

hey
i think you're really cool
i like you a lot
maybe we can hang out
or something

my friends and i
love this dance
called
the nae nae
and so
whenever we hit it
it's pretty crazy :0

don't ever tell me
i'm ugly
cuz its
bitch is you blind

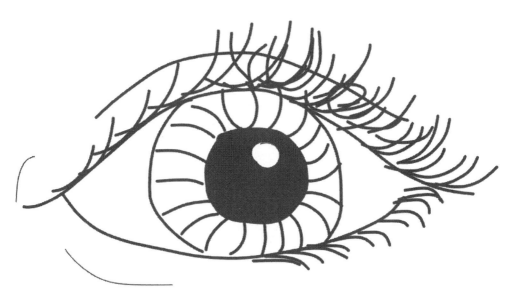

who's the hottest uber driver
you've ever had

um
i never went to
oovoo javer

jerry
jerry
i want you to
fuck me
jerry

psst

what

hey kayla
check out this face

oh my god
zach
i'm going to pee

what

zach i'm peeing

kayla
not on the
leather seats

i'm quitting vine
because somebody commented
on a post
saying i look like
a piece of broccoli
so goodbye
forever

shawty i
don't
mind

stop saying i look like
chicken little
he's dumb
and he's a coward
and i am not
a coward

okay
you know what
you're in time out
get on top of the fridge
get up there

this house is a
fucking nightmare

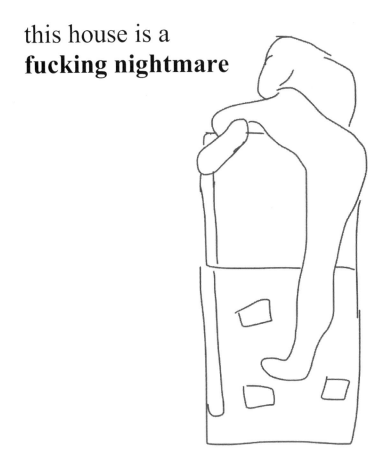

you know what
i'm about to say it

i don't care
that you broke your elbow

this is how
i enter my house

wassup fuckers

why do you have my phone

fuck you
that's why

not this guy again

dick
got some dick here
want some dick

he's just trying to feed his family

here i'll take two bud

hey
god bless ya man

marleen
your speech was
so good

oh cause like
i didn't even like try
it was just like improv

oh my god
why can't you just take
the freakin
compliment

hi

okay

dude
are you five

yeah
five inches deep
*in your **mom***

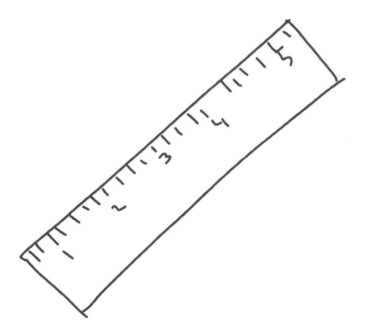

i'm over this dumbass school
with all these
fake ass people

hey

hey

fuckin bitch

you gawn get wehht
ayeeee aint gun
take you howme

awwwww come ownnn
he got his daymn feet weht
now shit-dawg

well
when life gives you
lemons

oh my gosh
is that corbin blue
from jump in

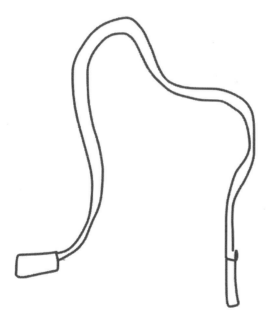

i figured out a way to
um
record without any hands
you do have to be a boy though
i'll figure out something for the
girls
in a lil bit

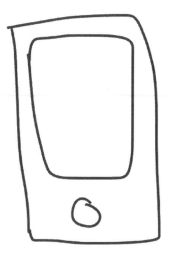

guys
just a little family announcement
i'm changing my birthday
to today
so

it's fucking christmas

really
you're going to be a dick to me
on my bday

dad
look
it's the good kush

this is the dollar store
how good can it be

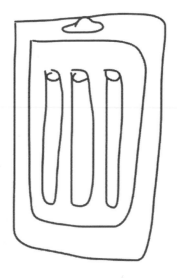

all i fucking wanted
was fucking bangs

what the fuck

hey how you much you pay
for that taco

ey yeah
you know what it is
boy's got his free taco

guess what i'm eating

popcoooooorn

can i get a waffle
can i please get a waffle

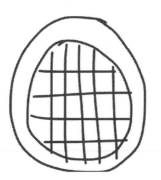

sounds like something she'd say

heuheuheuheuheuheuh

i like that laugh
heuheuheuheuh

i don't need friends
they disappoint me

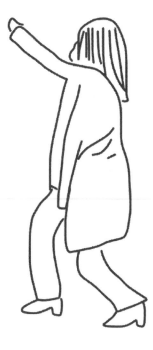

yo
what're we about to do

drink this vodka
down the hatch

got diagnosed with
cool guy syndrome yesterday
hahah
so i now
i take

adderall
hahhah

you stupid

no i not

what's 9+10

21

you stupid

heyyy
i want to be famous

skza

is it
is it real

look at these bumps
you got
egzma

i got what

you got
egzma

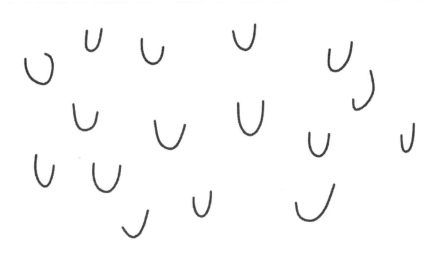

my mom said
if i don't get my grades up
she's not gonna let me
get my tetnus shot next year

that's weird
what are you gonna do

fucking study i guess

you know what
i love myself
even though i look like
a burnt chicken nugget
i still love myself

have y'all tried these
boys hot

back at it again
at krispy kreme

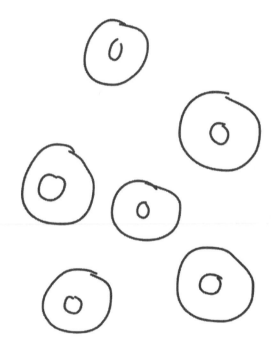

*i get more bitches than you
tho*

fuck no baby

i'm just
chilling
in cedar rapids

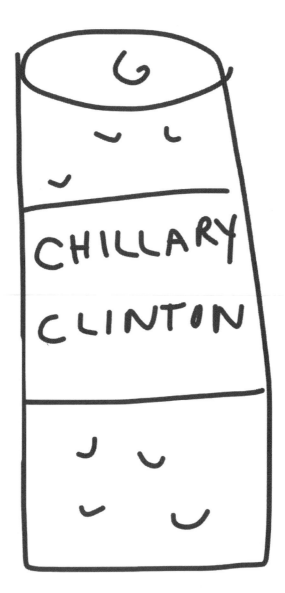

and after that he said
i wish you were never born
and
that's why i don't go home
for thanksgiving anymore

anyways
can i get a
double cheeseburger

achoo

nice ron

i sneezed
oh
i'm not allowed to sneeze

you

i mean
four
female ghost busters
the feminists
are taking over

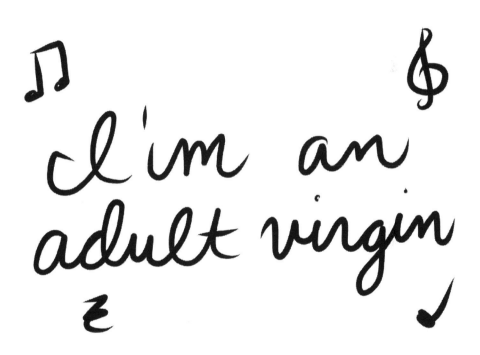

hi
i'm renata bliss
and i'm your
freestyle dance instructor

look at this

graph

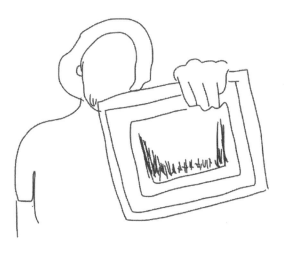

can you guys say
colorado

i'm a giraffe

do it for the vine

i ain gon do it

do it for the vine

i ain gon do it

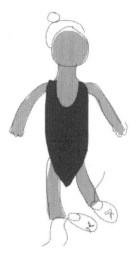

do it for the vine

i gon do it

first let me hop out the

porsche
i don't want to hit that

shut the

up

magcon is my bae
yeah
magcon is my day
yeah

lebron james
lebron james
lebron james
lebron james
lebron james

does it feel good

ah

wait
oh yes
wait a minute
mr. postman

eeeehhhhhaaaaeeehhhh

who am i
let's go to the beach beach

ninki minjaj

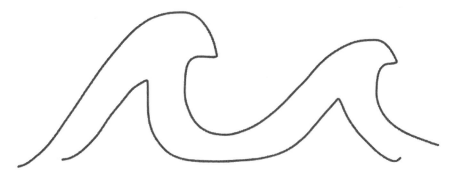

let me make this
friggin clear
i am not a friggin phase
live with it
parents

deez nuts
hah
got em

welcome to my kitchen
we have bananis
and avicados

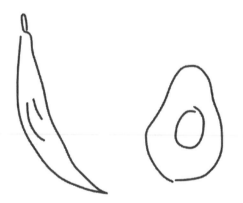

heyyyy hey hey
hey
kids kids

patricia

honey can you be quiet
i'm just trying to do
something

i love niall horan
with his blue eyes
and blonde hair
he make me do this

from the manatee county fair
linda carson
abc 7
would you not
eat my pants
ahhhhhh

it's me
jessie and ari
if he
if they test me
they sorry
ride his uh like a harley
then pull up in his ferrari

do you ever like
wake up
or do uh
like
do something
and you're just like
what the he–
fuck
is going on

so is like
this gooing to be a thing
me and you
uh
uh

mah dicc fell off

adam

Interested in more content?

Follow us on Twitter!
   @adam_gasiewski
   @emiilybeck

Check out our website at milkandvine.org for updates and cool merch!

Subscribe to our YouTube channel Milk and Vine for interviews, compilations, and more!

Acknowledgments

Thank you for reading our tribute to the late and great Vine app. We wholeheartedly thank all of the vine creators who made this amazing content.

Page 14: Katy Perry @katyperry
Page 15: Tai Habersham @taibernacle
Page 16: its just luke @its_just_luke_
Page 17: Casey Frey @freycasey
Page 18: Matt Sukkar @MattSukkar
Page 19: LisaMolly @LisaMolly_
Page 20: mielmonster @miel
Page 21: Jimmy Ustar @jimboslice7197
Page 22: Brandon Rogers @brandonlovesyou
Page 23: Braith @braith

Page 24: Daniel Gomez @daniel_gomezzzz

Page 25: Bill Geralis @billgeralis

Page 26: Jean Chenet @jayhove_

Page 27: Kennedy Taylor @kennedytayl0r

Page 28: she_skin

Page 29: irham

Page 30: Jared Friedman @jared_friedman1

Page 31: Craig's Last

Page 32: Drew Gooden @drewisgooden

Page 33: Josh Kennedy @jjoshkennedyy

Page 34: Lorenzo Orsi @lorenzorsi

Page 35: jay_justchillin @jay_justchillin

Page 36: iJay_BE3 @iJay_BE3

Page 37: Katie Ryan @katieryan430

124

Page 70: Lilianna Hogan

Page 71: Unknown

Page 72: Jimmy Murrill
@JimmyMurrill

Page 73: Violated Memes

Page 74: uniladsnap

Page 75: Unknown

Page 76: Unknown

Page 77: Josh Kennedy @filmquaker

Page 78: kim kardASHLEY
@ashleymabry

Page 79: frieswithcheese
@frieswithcheese

Page 80: imchasen @imchasen

Page 81: Unknown

Page 82: Mightyduck

Page 83: Access Hollywood Interview

Page 84: ActingClassSarantos

Page 85: Jaden Jeffords

Page 86: Josh Kennedy @filmquaker

Page 87: BRUH @BruhVidz

Page 88: Rachel Olson

Page 89: Chari Sheen

Page 90: Isa

Page 91: Josh Kennedy
@jjoshkennedyy

Page 92: OMG its Richiey

Page 93: Zake @okitszake

Page 94: Aaron

Page 95: @dsususbdb

Page 96: Hillary Clinton
@HillaryClinton

Page 97: Cody Ko @codyko

Page 98: Wallum Cray

Page 99: Gabriel Gundacker
@Gabriel.Gundacker

Page 100: Fire In The Booth

Page 101: Euphemism for Magic

Page 102: Josh Wagner

Page 103: Dom @BrownnSkinn__

Page 104: Unknown

Page 105: Kk_Slays